When A King Of Hearts
Meets A Queen Of Diamonds

When A King Of Hearts Meets A Queen Of Diamonds

Playing your hand to win at "Relationships"

Paul Simms

To order additional copies of this book, contact:
Xlibris Corporation
1-888-795-4274
www.Xlibris.com
Orders@Xlibris.com
108610

DEDICATION

This book is very respectfully dedicated to a true friend, Mrs. Sherri Nicole Branch, a family woman who loves christ in her life, love's her family, her nursing career, and love's peace in everyone. She as a friend, has literally requested the book she knew I would write for over 30 years. Thank you for believing in me Mrs. Branch, I finally did it!!! . . . . May God bless you and your family!

SPECIAL THANKS

MR. LARRY D. Brown, my BIG BROTHER, and my best friend, thank you for always being there regardless as big brothers do. We've been through life like no other and have many stories that could be a book itself. A lot of what I learned from you is written in this book and you know it. I Love You Big Bro!

Thank you Mr. Robert Harris, a true friend who I will always respect and learn from, Thank you for being there after all these years.

To my sister Ms. Naima Alamin, you have many books within you, If you release just one, the world would be pleased! I Love You!

There are a lot of very special people in my life which makes it difficult to list them all, so I will say Thank You to all the personal friendships and relationships that meant a lot to me, you know who you are!!!

CONTENTS

INTRODUCTION

IT WAS A warm fall september 2010 afternoon as I sat in my work truck on a gravel lot in Muskogee, Oklahoma and the sun beamed brightly through the windshield of my truck, providing a comfortable warmth inside the cab and an extremely relaxing atmosphere when it hit me like a revelation, I have my book! I grabbed a blank piece of paper and a pen and I have'nt stopped writing since. I've always loved pen to paper and I still today excercise that method. Please allow me to give you some insight of the author. First and foremost Im a child of god, and to our father be all the glory! Im a son to my loving mother who passed the night of Sept 10th, 2001 the night before the terrorists attacks on 9/11 of the world trade center, and she could be desribed in one word, Momma! I love you mom, and your son has done well as you expected, thank you for being proud of me. I still have my father with me, going strong at 77yrs old and still holds a hero status with me. He has always been who I inspired to be like, a man of strength, a provider, and the funniest person I know. I love you Pops!

Im a father of two, and a true friend to only a few. My oldest is my son, who is my Jr., and who I will always Love and be there for if needed, has life in front of him and I will always want the best for him. My Babygirl, "Boogie", a talented young lady who is a true girly girl and love's life, Daddy loves you! As a 9 yr old, I grew up loving sports and playing baseball and attended college on a baseball scholarship after graduating high school. Im a dedicated KC Chiefs football fan so Im used to the ups and downs in relationships. I've been married once and have had many short term relationships which led to me learning that commitment actually has meaning. Acceptance also became important as I gravitated directly to accountability in my life. Working in the transportation industry the last 20 plus years, I've been exposed to quite a bit in life and took many notes along the way. I joined the United States Navy in my mid twenties and basicly have been blessed to meet a lot of people along the way in life. My values and standards stems from my parents hard work mentalities, their strength, and my awareness of what I've been taught in life.

My reasons and goals for writing my book was simple for me, I just wanted to help anyone I could, have a better relationship and be content and enjoy life as I do. I've had this dream of writing my book since high school, and this one particular friend would never cease reminding me to write my book. And then by coincidence, a co-worker informed me that he had just became published and it inspired me as well. I purchased his book, (Love's Insanity . . . A Poetic Diary) by King Emanuell, which is available through Xlibris Publishing.com, and two plus two was beginning to equal four. I was at the time having numerous conversations from all angles about relationships, so the genre was automatic. Since elementary I loved to read and write and the book within me was noticed by several during high school who encouraged me to write. I had the interest all the time, but at 50 yrs old, you can see I progressed with the blazing speed of a tired snail, 30 yrs later. It finally became important to me, and as they say, It shall be written, It shall be done!

CHAPTER 1

Playing to Win

H E'S A KING of hearts, your highness, soon to be your majesty, a ladies' man, a smooth operator, and the type of man a woman finds herself captured by once he sprinkles words of charm all over her. Some women wanna say no, but it's now too late; curiosity is about to kill the cat, or at least, caress it properly.

She's a Queen of diamonds, a woman of class, a sculptured feminine goddess of beauty, intelligence, and independence; and she sparkles with desire. She makes men pause as she keeps it moving, staying focused, knowing in her heart and mind that she will submit into the hands of the best diamond sculptor, the man soon to be her King.

The moment they meet and eye contact is made, a feeling flows through their bodies that produces a variety of, and a multitude of, thoughts and reactions. Curse words, spiritual clichés, and body language dictate the moment of truth. The King of hearts is anticipating the "it's all good" signal of a flirtatious smile, a sign of shyness, or eyes that say, "Come here, boy!" The Queen's extremely swift examination of that man from head to toe—his hair, smile, physique, and footwear (and size)—begins the approval or disapproval rating, and now his approach, greeting, and deliverance of that greeting she anticipates. Let the games begin!

Playing your hand to win at relationships is exactly that; meaning, that if you want to win, you want success. Plan B is not an option here; simply doing the right thing is all that applies. Common sense, experience, and a desire and commitment to do the right thing will deal you a good hand, but how you play that hand is entirely up to you.

What separates a marriage from a relationship? A tree, ink, and a gavel!

I've always admired and respected longevity in relationships. Long-term marriages are like one of the greatest accomplishments we can have, and a true inspiration in relation to relationships for me to write about. I've been asked numerous times, "How can you write about marriage and relationships and you're single?" Well, the fact is, I'm not writing about marriage, but I do have plenty of relationship experience. The truest form of marriage in my opinion, though, is genuine and true commitment. Anyone can be together for years, but how real the commitment is describes the value of that relationship. Through the good and the bad, time will tell and test your commitment. There are not really any excuses for being wrong to your partner, there are only reasons. It's a matter of being accountable for your actions. One partner in that relationship has to be stronger than the other at certain points, so the aspect of being teammates, of teamwork, the "we're in this thing together to the end," will be tested to its limits. Not giving up on a relationship or marriage is playing to win "if" you're not blinded by a commitment that does not have your best interest at heart.

"Don't assume commitment," establish it! Sex is not commitment; sex is sex. For a woman to give herself sexually to bond with a man for the purpose of commitment and exclusivity, she must be very clear about her expectations and his intentions, and she must hope for the best possible outcome.

For men who are playing to win, first and foremost, just be a man. It will require truth and accountability and all that you have to be a genuine leader of your family. Playing to win doesn't mean that life is a game; what I'm trying to say is that life can be competitive, so compete with it while having a strategy to win at the success/failure aspect of life and remembering the whole time that you're part of a team, even when your teammate is not at their best and makes mistakes. The subtitle, playing your hand to win at relationships, speaks clearly about handling your business as a man, knowing you hold the trump card and won't be cut out of the game. There are many aspects to developing a successful relationship, and one very important one is knowing what you want. If you've made yourself important first, chances are excellent that you have a solid idea of what you prefer in life. And for whom this applies to, stop freelancing through life without real purpose and find something to be good at and proud of, and live it. It doesn't matter if it's running a small business, physical fitness, obtaining wealth, playing pool, bowling, sex, employment, or a hobby. What actually happens is you began to find worthwhile purpose in a meaningful part of your life and your self-worth gives you inspiration for importance in other areas of your life, hopefully your relationships. You have to begin somewhere, so try with a choice you will put your all in. For an example, if it's about sex, learn how to have sex responsibly and with passion. Just know that you can't satisfy everyone, but you don't have to. There's a difference between making love and having sex, and it has everything to do with who's to be satisfied the most and taking your time to do it right. Making love is personal; having sex is simply having fun. When you're playing to win, you will do either one at the appropriate time when needed.

I've been labeled as a married man, a player, a sexual man, a whore, a committed man, marriage material, irresistible, noncommittal, don't know what I want, and one of a kind. If Chaka Khan is every woman, then I'm every damn man! I consider myself a ladies' man because of my love, because of my weakness, and because of my strength for women; and I can appreciate being in love. Truth, honesty, and accountability are what I use personally as my guide to playing to win, regardless of how I'm perceived or known.

Playing to win means that if you have a true friend in your relationship, you should take advantage of that and build on it because "real" friendship has love written all over it. The mirror is for more than grooming, so try to understand and accept what you really and truly have. As friends, you trust and rely on each other and know that as a team, all is possible. People can read a book or hold conversations all day long about doing things better and then go on with everyday life and never apply any of it. When the situation presents itself, "play to win" in the life you live by simply doing the simple things that will help you come up. Save money, go to school, spend money on things that matter, prepare and plan your future whether it's short term or long term. Become serious about being in your relationship, or don't begin one unless you're gonna be for real.

Learning how to build a strong foundation requires learning from those who have lived life thoroughly. Confide in couples who have many, many years of togetherness in marriage or friendship and ask about specific opinions such as truth, respect, change, compatibility, adjustments, acceptance, love, and flaws. One good piece of advice, listen carefully with your ears and not with your mouth, and don't interrupt while grown folks are teaching. For those who teach us and for those who genuinely care about us for whatever reasons, they will literally give us the best opinions they possibly can offer. Those relationships that began early in life and last to see a fiftieth anniversary are classic examples of life's relationships lessons. Being together consistently that long automatically gives you lessons to teach others about. The good, the bad, the ugly, the glory, the pain, the love and the hate, the mistakes and the praise, you've grown together and have shared life to an extreme level of oneness that others could only imagine. Those are the ones you can learn from even though they don't have educational degrees in the field of relationships.

When developing relationships for success, please have reasonable expectations; meaning, don't truly expect someone else to treat you better in life than you treat yourself. If you treat yourself with a level 6 grade of importance (with 10 being the best), and you want your partner to treat you with a minimum level 9 grade of importance, who are you truly being fair to, and who does it truly benefit? It's no different than if you get with someone and they have it going on pretty damn good because of the hard work they've put in, you will respect them and know that you will probably have to have your game together in order to be with them. So basically, be considerate with your expectations and analyze the whole situation, being fair to them as well as yourself. Instead of making assumptions or guessing about who you're dealing with, be as nosy as possible, and I don't mean spying or asking questions showing jealousy. Ask your partner "why" questions, similar to the grilling by a two-year-old, learning why they really have you in their life and how can "we" do it better. A lot of people in relationships have never asked important questions that they may wonder about, so they never truly know the answers to those questions that lie within them. Make important the exposure of true intentions; meaning, fellas, if you are who you say you are, then why lie and front with fake game. Some men don't understand that being real is the best way for success; women love it. Even if sex is all you want, don't hesitate to make that clear, and don't take every single option off the table, time can bring about change.

In my research, the responses I've received from people depended on how they actually felt at that moment in their lives and was according to their mood as well that day. Marriage was either real good, or it was real bad. You see, relationships don't change, people change within relationships. I can ask the same person similar or the same questions three to five different times and receive three to five different perspectives depending on where they're at in that moment. Playing to win is using rational thinking and truth and accepting what truly comes with your personal situation. In order to achieve success and enjoy success, you must have a plan and strategy that benefits you and your partner. Teams win together, and they fail together; it's all in how you construct and direct your path for success individually and collectively, with the end result being peace, harmony, respect, love, and togetherness.

You can truly find many successful marriages and relationships to gauge how success can be achieved despite all the negative information you may hear, read, or see. Playing to win by the King of hearts and the Queen of diamonds has been achieved tenfold, so now, how will you play your hand?

Capture Her

T HE LOVEABLE AND adorable women of this world have a best friend: diamonds! For those who are not aware, there are four Cs that make up the existence of such a precious stone. Cut, clarity, color, and cost define the diamond she holds dearly as it makes her sparkle as well. In part of my attempt to define relationships, I've come up with my set of four Cs men go through in the relationship process. They are capture, celebrate, commitment, and conundrum. It's amazing what a man will do or attempt to go through to meet, greet, treat, and be sweet to God's gift to man—woman! Although all men are not the same behaviorally, and we have different approaches to women, the goal is the same, capturing our prize. It's all in the hunt, and to capture her is golden!

As I make eye contact, I manufacture a look of desire, respect, and lust as smoothly as a true ladies' man is capable of. To capture her is to create something new for her, something she's never had before: Me! She doesn't know what she could possibly have with me, but I will provide all she needs to understand that. She now becomes increasingly important to me, and I shall make her totally aware of my intentions, hoping for acceptance without a major deterrent. Whatever a man's motivation shall be, to capture her can turn out to be a lifetime achievement. We try to capture dreams sometimes in life, and certain women can make men mature quicker and achieve great heights, which in turn, he becomes her dream maker.

Whether it's at a store, Laundromat, school, work, bar, or stoplight, we've admired, analyzed, strategized, planned, lusted, regained composure, developed plan B, and moved in for the capture, all within sixty seconds. The success rate can only be measured by the type of man who loves being a man and finds capturing a woman's attention, her time, her smile, and her heart very important. The fact that the friendship is brand new adds an automatic rich excitement because of the unknown, the desired expectations, results, or outcome after the capture has been made. One positive about being a man is the ability to visualize a woman and then feel within ourselves some of the purpose in which God intended such as attraction and desire, which helps make capturing her such a great accomplishment. The beauty of the hunt is what keeps the hearts and minds of men motivated and stimulated for perfect execution in order to capture her. In reality, men believe they're actually doing the choosing, and we do to a point, but after a woman has been approached numerous times, she then will decide who the "chosen one" will be. It's really a competition some men are not aware they're a part of. Women take the time to appear as beautiful as a brand-new day (the present), and a true flirtatious man with confidence and courage as part of his basic DNA make-up approach women regularly, and a sweet sounding "hello" with a smile to acknowledge him is very rewarding.

It's actually the way that I ask for her—without saying a word, not being to proud to beg you see, and I've made up my mind that I'm coming to capture you, baby doll, and there's absolutely no defense for what I have in store for you. I enjoy a good challenge, so being refused in the beginning doesn't change anything unless "I" decide it that way. Oh no! I'm not arrogant, I'm just a very confident man. I love it when women tell me later on that I didn't stand a chance in the beginning, or their perception of me lacked all that I currently provide her now, and I laugh as they now call me Big Daddy! I've captured women in many different fashions, so the process actually does depend on the moment. I've been bold and confident, giving respectful but demanding requests, taking only yes for responses, and while at other moments been a submissive slave to certain women. Some men would go to great lengths to be with certain women, going all out financially and emotionally and end up setting themselves back but enjoying the ride while it lasted. The cliché "We spend nine months trying to come out of the cocoon, and then spend the rest of our lives trying to get back in it" has never been more true. A man can genuinely appreciate a woman's gentle touch in a simple conversational gesture such as a hand on our chest, arms, or shoulders, or a handshake that can send chills. Mentally or verbally, we will say, "Damn, you're so soft," and we won't forget that unconscious or conscious display of affection. The power of a woman is a gift from God, to bring men down from their high testosteronial horse and relax, to soothe the savage beast so to speak.

In order to capture her, you first must approach her, so let's discuss how we can handle this situation. How a man approaches a woman successfully is an art form women appreciate and anticipate. You must be smooth, cool, calm, and collected, exuding confidence to let her know her King is present. Be yourself, not someone you think she wants you to be. Most women can spot fake sincerity but will play along if you're charming, funny, and sweet to them. "Game recognizes game," so stay in your lane and be yourself, trust me on this one. The first important accomplishment in your approach should be to "establish a comfort level," by having a respectful tone in your voice, a calmness in your demeanor, and saying what's in your heart. Making a woman comfortable is an instinctive male responsibility, and women truly desire that in men. When you have her attention, direct eye contact is important; the eyes say a lot. The awakening of particular emotions to make her smile is important, so producing a smile from her is the second important accomplishment to strive for. Every woman should smile every day, and it's our duty to help get the job done. It's fairly easy if she's feeling pretty, sexy, and flirtatious; the fun part is getting her to smile if the moment is challenging. One of the most beautiful moments in life for a man is when a woman that a man wants to capture actually wants to be captured by him. It's a beautiful thing when the hunter becomes the hunted in these cases—God is good! Some of the tools used for a successful approach includes an old-fashioned flirtatious wink, sending a cocktail with a message, eye contact with strategy, using babies or pets, or just simply jumping in and making a purchase for her she was about to purchase herself: "I'll take care of that for her." If she's flattered by the hard work and effort you put in trying to impress her, you may be good to go at that point. It's actually a natural part of my DNA to acknowledge women simply because "I have to." A manufactured gentle hello to women will also work to get her attention, but remember, it's not that you said hello, it's how it's delivered. Body language can define emotions as well as certain behaviors; it's all in the technique you use.

Let a woman know when she has that wow factor going on because a woman can appreciate genuine attentive flirtatious compliments. Don't just tell her she looks good; give her credit for what directly appeals to you and how you notice the sexiness. If you want to know if you've truly captured her, take notice of who ends the conversation first and why. If she stands before you and positions herself in a comfortable two-point stance with deep eye contact and a blush or smile on top of it, go buy a lottery ticket because you just might hit the jackpot twice in a day!

PAUL SIMMS

I'm the kind of man who, when I get excited about a woman, I tend to lick my lips over and over again as if they are secreting her sweet nectar already. The smoothest of the smooth guys have experience in the moment to speak off the cuff, and smiles are automatic for them. In order to capture her, let her know that all that matters at that point is her, making the focus on you two absolute as if no one else exists around you. If she reciprocates your flirting with her own and she's inquiring about you, she may have made her mind up. Women can know quickly if they're interested before you even have a clue. Being a gentleman, being punctual, and doing exactly what you say you're going to do goes a long way. The second or third meeting can truly solidify the capture process because there is no second or third if the first was a disaster; the process of communication is at it's early stages at this point, so a man should use his listening skills to his best ability, allowing her to express herself, her expectations, and what it will take to work. Continue to stay natural in your conversation so she gets to know the real you. Don't get too personal early; instead, search for her interests and values. There are huge rewards for patience, respect, consideration, and the possibility of a positive future that you as a man can offer.

Being the aggressive type of man is cool as long as it's regulated. Confidence should be the regulator of being aggressive, and most women will accept that. Contrary to the aggressive type of man, the laid-back, low-key kind of guy who has an aura of stability, confidence, and power, can be very sexy to women and intimidating as well. A true man of power never has to flaunt it. His swagger is genuinely obvious without hollering, "Hey, look at me." He's again, smooth, cool, calm, and collected, being a man of values and standards with principles who will not accept just any woman in his circle. She must and will be chosen in particular. Keep in mind, fellas, to make eye contact and keep it there as I mentioned previously, you can visually explore her body as she looks away. Using that maneuver, you intentionally want to get caught looking at her body as she returns eye contact; trust me, she won't be mad at cha! Intrusive eye contact digs deep to the soul sometimes, so she will respond to it. An old-school cat once told me, "If you get 'em kicking rocks, you got 'em!" How you present yourself helps make her decision, so speak firmly but pleasantly while manufacturing a grown-man level of maturity, being able to handle minor rejection. There's no need to act immature because women are not obligated to be receptive as you may prefer. Women get hit on all the time in some shape, form, or fashion; and it can be a hassle sometimes. I tell myself, women are like stars in the sky, you can't count them all. World statistics show that there are more women than men anyway, so breathe easy, fellas. If it were reversed, and men were getting hit on by women every day knowing they only want one thing would be heaven sent, and I could not wait to leave the house. Only the famous, rich, or extremely good-looking guys experience something similar, and for those men with that problem, God bless ya!

As a man reaches the most mature part of his life, capturing her has real purpose, constructive meaning, and exact reasoning that truly makes his focus as sharp as an eagle when it is zoned in to capture its prey. If you're already in a relationship or marriage, then recapture her. To my fellas working on it, if there's a woman you've had your eye on and you would love to begin the four Cs process, keep in mind that Kings conquer, Kings rule, and Kings capture, but don't get it twisted fellas Kings sometimes get overthrown, so don't take the success of your capture for granted because you know what they say, easy come, easy go! If you get her right, treat her right.

Capturing her, the first of the four Cs, might just be the beginning of what could be something special.

CHAPTER 2 "SECTION 2"

Celebrate Her

THE BEGINNING OF something real is definitely worthy of celebration, and the second of the four Cs, celebrate her, means that the King of hearts has claimed his Queen of diamonds and will now show his appreciation. You're celebrating what is considered a blessing, a gift, and the ability to become close and personal with someone only a chosen few will ever know in this manner. After a grand accomplishment such as capturing her, celebrating this accomplishment is truly all about her, or at least 90 percent of it, the other 10 is for my glory.

She's so beautiful, it's like God sent her on a path to meet you. You're fascinated by her looks, how she walks, smiles, carries herself like a lady, how she feels, smells, and tastes. Celebrating her can make a man daydream at times. "What you thinking 'bout, man?" is what you'll hear, and you'll respond after that big smile crosses your face, "Ahh, I'm good, man!" When a man looks at his new friend and thinks, "Damn, she makes me look good," then celebrating her is so very easy to do. Celebrating her is to cherish her, to admire her, and to appreciate her. A very cool vibe between men is when we say, "Man, I wanna be like you," and that's after we see who's on their arm in these cases. God created woman for the purpose of companionship with man for many reasons, and those purposes tend to become crystal clear at this stage. You know she has hopes and desires to one day meet that one man who will be the one who stabilizes and completes her life and future with her own family and real-life fairy-tale story. As her new friend, you can't guarantee that at this point, but it's one step at a time and a time to celebrate the beginning.

As men, we walk with that pride, confidence, and assurance that the woman we're with is secured and protected by us. She's my Queen, and I shall defend her to the end. No problem, I will walk proud like "Yeah, she's with me! It's just a man thing of being territorial. There are approximately two to three billion men on planet Earth, and she chose you to be the man in her life, so celebrate her. At this point, she probably takes up 50 percent of your daily thoughts from the moment you awake until you fall asleep again. That's actually good for the heart, mind, body, and soul. Positive thinking and positive feelings promote more positive results in other areas of your life.

Celebrating her can come in many forms. To simply stare at her, and this may actually sound simple, but this form of admiration will expose the type of emotions that will make her blush childishly. In celebration, you claim, "That's my baby! Ain't she fine? If anything but a positive response is returned, I'll pay $1,000 for a snapshot of the look on your face when you hear something negative. Hating on our celebrating is unacceptable because the end of the ride is no where in sight! "Let me get that for you, baby!" is the norm during celebrating. A man is fulfilled when he speaks of her, speaking proudly, assured, climactically, and with conviction.

When celebrating her and you're representing her, dress the part, you're representing for two now. Doing the little things for a woman makes her have appreciation from the deep part of her heart, such as a foot massage without her asking or having a hot bubble bath ready after work just because. You keep "your" ride clean, have hers detailed without her knowledge, or let her find or walk up on something that says you've missed her or love her. I've walked hand in hand with women having moments in my life feeling like the baddest MF walking simply because I was with her. One of the best times of relationships is the beginning for sure because of the sharing. You want her to feel the same good feelings you may encounter regardless of what they are because she's in your heart, and you're feeling her for real. If you're the type of man who has no clue what sharing is all about for real, you do at this point in relationships because of its feel good moments. You can enjoy life's simple things like sharing a movie, conversation, short weekend getaways, scenic views, and hobbies. And as you share them with her, she gains more importance after each time shared because you're celebrating her every time.

When it's time to share her, the ultimate introduction as we all know is to our parents, and the acceptance from our best friends has serious meaning as well. The mind and heart function intensely with the anticipation of meeting with our loved ones because of the expectations of acceptance from them. A lot of relationships are from models of our parents' relationships, but life has its twists and turns, and it doesn't necessarily work out that way. But when meeting our partner's parents, afterward the question is automatic: "What did your mom/dad think of me?" The involvement of others in this new relationship expands the spectrum so to speak while all we want is to be accepted. I personally enjoy seeing couples that seem good together, having fun and appearing inseparable. Even if I don't know the inner workings of their relationship, I admire what it appears to be, especially with senior couples. Our mothers are the first to nurture us, and our first relationship begins, then we get advanced relationship lessons from our girlfriends and the likes telling us exactly how it works. One thing I learned as a young man was how it turned me on when women blushed and smiled and showed a shy side. Women's beautiful eyes and smiles began to mesmerize me at a young age, and that hasn't changed to this day. There's nothing to compare to how a woman can make a man feel, act, think, and behave. When he meets that one particular woman, and there are no clues for her arrival, you can stick a fork in him because he is done!

A man loves the feeling of seeing his new baby approaching him knowing she's his and she's coming to see him. The embrace, the gentle kiss, and the eye contact shows we've got it goin' on for real. Although it may be early in the relationship process, celebrate her during special moments such as birthdays, Valentine's Day, Christmas, and most importantly, just because, remembering at the same time the reason she attracted you in the first place. During the course of relationships, she could be difficult at times, but she's God's angel for real, and a woman that's meant to be celebrated by her man. Celebrate her by being on time, keeping your word, participating in her interests, including her in your interests, and if you can cook, preparing her a meal with an aviaunce she will appreciate. The "just because" gifts and the time you spend show her how important she is to you while you accumulate brownie points as well. Women truly want to be shown that they're loved and appreciated, so don't pass up the opportunity when the thought or moments arise. A simple phone call out of nowhere to say "I love you" and "All that you have meant to me" in a sixty-second moment will last forever. Gifts that accentuate her career or schooling are thoughtful and shows an interest in what's important to her. It truly is the thoughtfulness, and you don't have to go broke to do it. I'm the kind of man who takes pride in being strong mentally as well as physically, but I do understand that women have the ability to affect men in ways that you have to make adjustments and changes for. I'm also the type of man who will let a woman know how they're in control in the beginning, but a transfer of power is inevitable.

Women normally choose the man they feel right about, but as men, we are strong in confidence and full of purpose and will not be denied that woman that changes us. Even the most promiscuous of men can be brought to a complete halt when the right woman appears in his life.

At some point during the celebration process, we acknowledge the one, and to some, the most intriguing aspect of celebrating is the anticipation and the actual moment of intimacy. If you're a man playing chess, "King Me" would be the appropriate term used to describe his manhood at that moment. Intimacy in any form can be emotionally powerful, either passionate lovemaking, wild sex, or hot steamy caressing, a woman still holds the power to make a man behave because we know how rewarding behaving can be. It's better to give than to receive when learning how to make love. It's knowing how and when to give and how and when to receive. You celebrate her slowly and attentively, stopping to capitalize on any area she shows signs of weakness, celebrating her with a firm but gentle touch. Men, please pay attention and understand that foreplay is very important to women, so a considerable amount of passion during foreplay is highly recommended. A woman wants to be led to the promise land of lovemaking with a head-to-toe appreciation of her body and mind. The mental foreplay is the serious aspect of "emotional releasing," so get ready for the ride, my brotha, and be prepared to "put it down" with a purpose at that point. As an example of administering passion, I'm a weakling for lemon cake with lemon icing. In saying that, as I bite into that slice, I first visualize it before I fall prey to indulgence, saying to myself, "Come to big papa!" I close my eyes, I embrace the feeling it gives me, and I slow life down momentarily in order to enjoy it as if it may never return. I savor the flavor as it puts my mind in a state of ecstasy. Damn, that cake tastes good! All I'm saying, fellas, is please give similar attention to her during the intimate moments of celebrating her.

The celebration of a woman by a man is a resemblance of appreciation from man to God, saying thank you for bringing her into my life. Celebrating her teaches others how to respect, love, and care for their partner in a relationship. Our children are paying attention to us, and when they see a man treat a woman right, they learn from it, hoping that happiness comes their way in the same manner. After a man captures a woman and she has given him permission to be the man in her life, it's our responsibility to celebrate her. If the celebrating lasts, there's a next step designed to conceal the deal for preparation to its final destination. Commitment to her is the next level of communication to prove you're her King and she is your Queen.

Commitment to Her

YOU HAVE OFFICIALLY passed all or the majority of your first round of tests, and yes, sir, I did say first round. It's time to take serious up a notch. Has the balance of power shifted yet, or is she still in control at this point? A lot of men can't spell commitment, less known, actually commit to it. It's easier to do though when you're on cloud nine about your lady, but when a reality moment kicks in, it can be similar to a man being bitchsmacked for real. Genuine commitment is truly a beautiful thing if you're agreeing to commit with a woman you're for sure about. If you tell your family and friends that you're interested in a serious commitment or a relationship and they start laughing, you may have commitment issues.

Fellas, just be careful how you word your commitment to her and use truth, honesty, and real talk. Realize and understand that we're not done making mistakes, and just because your woman is super fine and she's good to you, don't tell her you just decided to become perfect; it ain't gonna happen. We truly need to understand the importance of, and the reasoning for, committing. The type of communication to develop a genuine understanding is defined by quality. Celebrating her is not over yet; it has just taken on new meaning if the two of you decide to commit to exclusivity. I'm currently a single man, and when asked why I'm single, I always have a couple of truthful answers. I am single because at this stage in my life, I take commitment very seriously. The other reason is that I'm not in love, and I'm tired of the one-or two-year stints, and it's over. The truth within me tells me to quit wasting my time and be serious with me first, then with her.

Commitment has no specific concrete boundaries of longevity, quality, sincerity or range. Your commitment is what you make it and how you execute its outcome. Responsible men generally have responsible commitments, and the opposite usually always have issues. If you're going to commit, what are you committing to? A real commitment to a woman, in all reality, is like a gift. You're not doing her any favors or helping her out; you're purposely obligating yourself to a real-life bond where trust and dependability means everything. You obviously saw something in her or about her that you don't want to get away, so agreeing to become one with her means she must have put that "act right" on ya in whatever shape, form, or fashion, and now what's a man to do. Don't play with her heart or emotions in the same realm that you don't want anybody playing with your money. And you know how a man is about his money. I've had conversation at the beginnings of new friendships with women about noncommitment, believing and thinking we understood that commitment was not an option for me, only to have it challenged later as if it was never understood. As a man, you owe it to a woman to specify your true intentions with clarity.

For the men who are scared of commitment, it's not as bad as it's negative reputation or your assumptions. Commitment can actually bring about solid security, comfort or dependability, increased worth, shared responsibilities, additional knowledge, valuable support, and balance in your life. Men probably function better unbalanced, but we can adjust to being balanced. Commitment can be like drinking liquid medication—you know it's good for you, it's just the initial taste and the aftertaste that's scary. One of the beautiful things of being committed is the multiple reminders of why you're with her. How and when she gets out of the car and you watch her walk away, you think, "Damn, I'm hittin' that, and whenever I want!"

Some relationships are defined simply by either sex, money, infatuation, spirituality, children, true love, drugs, education, or an anticipated secure future to name a few. Using infatuation as an example, those who believe it's love and it's actually infatuation will be committing for the wrong reason. If you actually take the time to learn who you're dealing with and talk about your willingness to accept one's flaws, family, employment, hobbies, personality, and behaviors, you can then begin building a constructive foundation. When commitment is made without knowing the answers to the questions of an organized profile, then who are you really committing to. Fellas, if the doctor gives you a prescription for common sense, don't fill it with the generic brand. Commitment involves more than just yourself and your partner when there are children involved. It's also wise and recommended to never pass on what you feel is right for you in fear of commitment. Ask her to be patient with you while you make a "real" decision to become exclusive. If you're ready and you know it, communicate the direction for the future you have in mind. Committing as adults deal with real feelings, so playing games is wrong from the start. If you're considering commitment, and there's hesitation on your part, let truth and honesty become known. Giving up our freedom as men can be confusing, but a man in love does not give a shit about losing his freedom.

If you're just being selfish and it's all about you, then change the dynamics from commitment to friend with benefits. In other words, quit bullshitting! Relationships or families formed for the wrong reasons will be functioning for the wrong reasons with a future that's only temporary. Relationships are formed and molded based upon hard work and balance to solidify a potentially great union, which involves everyday effort to do the right thing. For a man, the foundation of commitment begins with you and your words and actions. A happy marriage is the ultimate goal of commitment, but actually living together in a committed relationship also requires dependency, trust, honor, faith, and teamwork. One key element to a successful relationship is to be true to yourself. "To thine ownself be true" is the great quote that helps to bond a great partnership. Within that partnership, sacrifice is not a burden, and selfishness makes one uncomfortable. Happy couples function with their daily duties without mentally convincing themselves they have to do them.

Partners listen to be a soundboard and ask about their partners everyday issues to help solve a problem, working as a team. They participate in each others' interests and also allow space so that they can be themselves. The result is a comfort level that includes accepting one's bad breath, the funky aroma of a no. 2 situation, and breaking wind without retreating. You wanna talk about love! I have admiration for real commitment because of the reality of the giving of one's self totally with longevity. For those men who have stayed faithful in a marriage with longevity, you're a rare breed. My father's marriage, approaching fifty years, has shown me longevity and the meaning of sticking in there through thick and thin. Although my dad is not a perfect man, I'm proud of him and idolize him and actually take after him in many ways, yet he and I are different when it comes to relationship commitment.

One reality to understand as a man when committing is the purpose of a man in a relationship. The early stage is where you make very important decisions, with the first one being the actual acceptance of a commitment. The quality you instill or the lack of quality defines your seriousness. If you're not bringing anything positive to the table, why would you expect any positive results to come of your relationship? As boys, the boyfriend-girlfriend togetherness was cute, cool, and interesting, but as men, the circumstances are real. We become husbands, fathers, teachers, providers, protectors, problem solvers, and more—the dependability level rises dramatically, and some of us as men don't recognize or consider it seriously. Decisions financially, spiritually, and all areas of family life all depend on you and her. A man is to be the leader in his family, plain pure and simple. Man did not make these rules; we're just here to follow them. If anyone tells you differently, then let the power struggle begin with them and God. But as a man, handle your responsibilities within a commitment. Man was not put on earth to be master of his family as a slave owner, so respect to your wife and children is mandatory, but be the leader and demand that respect as such. A man who divides his manhood does not deserve to be head of his family. Sharing responsibilities of the everyday functions does not constitute sharing power. Men and women both have their responsibilities in relationships, and upon committing, a quality understanding really solidifies where you both stand. The communication of togetherness and teamwork in the beginning is very important while trying not to allow division with petty power struggles. Women truly want a man to be "the man" because they know men were born to be leaders and having a real man is what they truly desire. It's hard enough being a woman in this world itself, so their expectations are valid in that area. Women should take their time allowing a man to be "the man" for their future if they don't truly respect all that he is. If it's the kind of relationship based upon getting your world rocked sexually, then let that be the reason. Relationships based upon good sex or good money are consistently temporary fixes for consistently momentary desires.

The Bone Fide Five

1. Be a leader—Come strong from day 1!
2. Be a provider—Be a Mr. Breadwinner.
3. Be a stabilizer—Bring stability or create it.
4. Be a protector—Be one at all costs.
5. Provide security—Secure your family's future.

A woman's heart is a very special place. It provides love, comfort, nurturing, sensitivity, understanding, and a place for two. God ergonomically placed love seats in the hearts of women, so when you find the right woman, take your time, relax and find out if her heart is a place where you can reside. When her heart is involved, she is not materialistic, plotting, or scheming to undermine; she is looking to become one with you in hopes that the future can be shared together. Do what's right and inform her if you have commitment issues that may be a problem. She may try to convince you that you are ready, but it is you who have to make that point crystal clear. She is not you, she wants to become one with you, so take charge and be responsible for your actions. Women sometimes commit with hope being their best friend if they hear what they want to hear and see potential in you. With commitment, a man should understand that women take being important very serious. She wants her importance to be recognized as priority one outside of her children and God in your life. She wants to be respected as Queen in your kingdom and treated as such.

A man's ex, mother, and adult children can be negative influences. If you "can't" put her in the category of Queen in front of family, friends, ex-women, and strangers, then a serious commitment is not recommended.

My truth and beliefs about noncommitment regarding men such as myself stands as this. My instinctive and natural born feeling, along with my developed reality and conclusion, is that one woman would not be satisfying enough over an undetermined period of time. That's the truth as I know and understand it, so it's easy to accept. I genuinely respect the discipline and willpower maintained in being monogamous. I'm not a follower so I can't be told or advised to follow anyone else's personal or social standards or values as if I believe them to be true. I'm true to myself and that shall never change. I also admit my lack of interest in working out issues where truth can't be prevalent. Disagreements with no or little meaning are a true sign of a lack of maturity, which will seriously limit my participation.

The fifty-fifty philosophy of men and women being equal is something I can't live by. I believe there is an order set forth we were created by, and we do not honor it based upon our own selfish ways we prefer to live. An obvious absence of our purpose here on earth has gotten far off the designed path. I believe men should be what women truly want them to be—leaders. That does not mean that men shall disrespect, disregard, control, or rule a woman as if she's incompetent. I've lived and experienced the intelligence of women, but no woman can be King of a castle; she obviously will rule as Queen if no King is present. A King of his castle will normally make decisions based upon his Queen's request's using her natural influence. With commitment comes the importance of sacrifice, restrictions, and compromise, which makes me state my stubbornness as a man to be selfish. If there is something I deem important, it will be done regardless, despite an undesired opposition. It truly takes an educated progression of maturity and intelligence for a man to be the accomplished leader of King a Queen can appreciate.

You've captured her, you've celebrated her, you've now committed to her, which means that there's a future to look forward to. She's a very special lady in your life now, or so says your commitment. If that part is not true, then what does your commitment really say then? Now we all know grown folks' commitment is totally different than children's commitment, or so I think, because kids seem to settle issues and play together quicker than us adults. But seriously, your commitment to her can lead to children, mortgages, car notes, and attorney fees, so make sure you're playing to win with a genuine commitment.

Commitment to her, number 3 of the four Cs, contains the power to make changes to your status. It's an agreement you should take seriously based upon the heart and mind, assumptions, fantasies, and discussions about the inevitable final destination, marriage. For some, it will be smooth sailing, and for the others, welcome to your conundrum!

CHAPTER 2 "SECTION 4"

Your Conundrum

FOR THOSE WHO are not familiar with the meaning, a *conundrum* is a situation that leaves you with only a guess for an answer. If a man has committed to a relationship knowing in his heart he won't be true to it, he has helped to create his own conundrum. A man can go from doing everything correct in his eyes and mind, to being told that what he does, how he does it, and who he does it with should change. Along the way, he encounters several relationship realities that teach him life's hard lessons, which brings him to the "make a decision" point. He will contemplate what relationship direction to go in, realizing he has arrived at his conundrum.

A woman can cause a conundrum in a man's mental psyche simply by being her emotional self. Women will tell you how to treat them at certain times such as "love me always, but not so much when, and don't treat me this way, but only if you, and give me space, but not that far, feel my emotions, now feel yours, but be a man, don't talk to me when, but understand I need you, I don't need you, because my, and when I'm, I love you, do you love me!" And after all that, she will look you straight in the eye and ask, "How can you not understand me?"

Women truly want strong men in their lives, men who handle situations swiftly, smartly, and with confidence, but when we put our proverbial foot down, like men should in relationships, some women can become very defensive. Challenging women for, or about power, is not what men look for. We're not criticizing or trying to belittle women, we're just being men of the house. Please understand, men who take advantage of women with a true lack of respect don't represent what men should be about. And for the women reading this section, please remember, "We're not perfect."

A man will generally give in to his woman if he knows she desires something badly, and she doesn't pressure him. It's extremely counterproductive to battle "against" the one that's on my team. To battle "with" is acceptable, but battling against does not improve progression and hurts stability. Trust and believe that the "first lady" has clout in the white house, she's confident that there's no need to prove she can be president too!

If we set goals for ourselves, why not set goals for your relationship? We find ourselves at the crossroads with our feelings after we've eventually become used to each other and that timing is usually one to three years. You're now trying to figure out if the faults you've recognized in the beginning are either adjustable, changeable, or if you should have that talk of being friends. Advice from family and friends, who just plainly seem to know more about your relationship than you, are in your ear when you're vulnerable and showing confusion or weakness. You tend to question yourself, "How did we come to this?" "How are you not who I envisioned you to be?" These are easy questions with difficult answers. You still want the relationship, but you don't want what comes with it at this particular time.

Women are very special beautiful creatures that God made for man's companionship, and we should cherish them as such. It really takes paying attention when being given good advice about how life in relationships can be so you're better prepared to handle the difficult times. To have confusion is good sometimes because it's like brain exercises to repair what's out of whack and to be put back into perspective. Thinking smart during difficult times makes you stronger in life and eventually defines your true mental strength. When our parents refused to help us as infants and toddlers, we began to learn problem solving, and as adults, we must educate and apply ourselves in the advanced degree. As a man, it's your responsibility to make sure that the woman in your life truly understands who you are, how you are, and what you are completely. In time, she will also know what you're capable of becoming. You two will need to discuss if she either accepts how you live your life or not. She really is waiting to hear and know your life's game plan for the direction you plan to lead your family in. She should, in turn, let you know if she's with you 100 percent, or that your best isn't good enough. Keep your eyes and ears, as well as your mind and heart, in focus to recognize how you're truly accepted. If you have a commitment worth giving your all, "Take your time and get it right, rather than rush it and get it wrong!"

The conundrum has begun because your answers to the issues and situations can change from minute to minute, hour to hour, day to day, and so on. Again, a clear lack of quality in communication is present, and maybe some selfishness has reared its ugly head. If you don't normally daydream, you probably do now. We all have been in this situation at some point; it's actually called the learning process. You've never wanted her to change, and hopefully she hasn't. You're actually just continuing to learn her. This is where truth and honesty becomes serious and important to administer in order to save, keep or redevelop a valuable relationship. Its how you manage the issues, situations, or confusion that really matters.

Failure speaks a foreign language that success just can't understand. Which one are you fluent in?

It's funny that there are relationships that exist where true love for one another defines the longevity, but the consummation for togetherness never took place. Distance between the two of you is natural in order to maintain harmony because not all couples can live together. Issues are inevitable, so clashing is normal, but the relationship will still last. These types of relationships reveal that improper emotional behavior dictates rational thinking and decision making, but true love wins in the end. Men say, "Women, can't live with them, can't live without them," knowing the latter is the truest. I was taught that if you treated your wife like you treated your best friend, maybe you would never separate. Friends seriously disagree and make up instantly, so imagine that type of functioning and instant forgiveness within your relationship. Marriages develop best friendships when longevity is present.

When real love marries, it doesn't get any better than that, but marrying for the wrong reasons seem normal. Fellas, if you want her to respect you, have her respect you for being strong and committed to what you "truly" believe in, whether she agrees with your beliefs or not. The relationship road may be bumpy at times, but nothing beats a try. The conundrum can be confusing not only from a commitment point, but the aspect of losing your freedom with commitment truly stands out in a man's mind. If there's any doubt that you won't be true to the situation, ask yourself why, evaluate the future, and don't hesitate being truthful and honest with yourself first. You may at one moment stare into her eyes and the thought may cross your mind, "How can something so good be a bad thing?" It's similar to forbidden food on a diet. The grass is not always greener on the other side, so don't throw away a potentially promising future.

If you truly get to the point of wanting genuine success in a relationship, then you should get serious in your approach to it. In general, we have relationships because of instinct, habit, and our desires to fill emptiness to name a few. We become confused in these relationships that have no designed positive purpose or direction because we fail to make ourselves important, our partners important, or the actual meaning of our relationship important. It's somewhat similar to the seriousness of religion and spirituality where some people only get serious when it's convenient or needed.

One relationship conundrum issue could be about a past relationship interfering with your current one. Have you ever wanted to be with someone so bad, but you couldn't have them? It can be torture being separated from a soul mate and best friend. In the form of a house, there's always a place for the past to come home to, a home of the heart. If you're to move forward, not only should you clean house, you have to bulldoze it of its existence. If you can always go back, you will, deleting all chances of progression. You can't throw true love away, but you do have the ability to move on with your life.

The conundrum stage of your relationship is the defining stage of its true existence to that point. Fellas, remember that the emotional heart of women needs to be pacified at times, and she needs to know that she is loved. Show her as well as tell her so she feels it. "A man simply wants to be respected, a woman simply wants to be loved."

Something to remember that's important is that appeasement never leaves your true feelings on the table; you're basically compromising or giving in to achieve peace instead of being true and real, and then you'll wonder why your partner doesn't truly understand where you're coming from. Just as computers need to be cleaned and cleared of viruses, so do our minds and hearts. Defragmentation of your mind allows you to clear up space to allow worthwhile data to be absorbed back into your head. Think of the concepts about your relationships that make you happy and write them down or store them in your head. Those are the activities or action moments that need to happen more or enhance those type actions with a new twist to keep the good vibes active. The things your partner enjoys in life are important to them so try to understand why. Being yourself or consuming yourself with what satisfies you allows you to be in a comfort zone as well, and maybe you can consider even joining your partner if you're not going to be critical or boring. Happiness does not just come up like the sun and moon; it must be created within originality and your own wishful and hopeful purposes.

We've heard the terms "successful relationship," "good relationship," and "perfect relationship." I will say they are so-called successful because it depends on what one considers successful. What kinds of people make such relationships happen? First of all, those who have come out of a conundrum with confidence, positive feelings, and a plan of solid direction. These are people who are genuinely in love, driven, self-respecting, accountable, and value—and standards-oriented with mental and emotional strength. Those who are driven always go through life functioning with purpose for future gain. Being accountable will exhibit no excuses, and an attitude of getting things done that will show progress and beneficial accomplishments. People who are standard and value oriented show self-respect and what's important in their lives, while demanding others respect them as well. The mental strength shows that you're not easily rattled, and all aspects about you are fortified.

I truly believe that fear of hurting one's feelings holds back the quality in communicating. When we talk as adults, we should be able to handle adult conversation, so hearing bad news is just a part of it. The feeling you have after cooler heads have prevailed is similar to being relaxed and satisfied after "extremely good sex." A smile will appear on your faces after the air is cleared and you've got it off your chest while experiencing a cool breeze of fresh atmosphere to live in after expressing yourself totally. If you're not able to walk away momentarily from confrontational issues, then ask for a "continuance" in order to handle the issue later. It's always better to clear the air right then and there, but it does not always work that way. The fact that you're actually looking to solve the issue at some point is always good. A lot of the mentality of the conundrum arrives from your relationship being based upon assumptions instead of concrete knowledge. When you see or sense something you disagree with or you're confused about, you then tend to just go through the motions assuming what the deal is.

If you fail to question your confusion or doubt, then you're only left to assume. Let your partner know that you're inquiring to achieve an understanding, just don't assume. You may wind up feeling a little silly when someone asks, "Well, did you ask this or that?" and you look puzzled and say something like, "No, I didn't, but I should have." That's part of the process of relationships that's called "working at it." Sounds simple, huh?

But you would be surprised. Communication is the key to relationship success.

Women will tell you what their expectations are and why they feel that way. They will assume that you will understand, agree, and follow suit with little logical resistance. The part that may cause a conundrum for men is that most of what women expect is logical, but not all of it. We're then forced to come out of simplicity and make decisions that require more than the normal amount of "feelings." Men don't operate on feelings unless there are women and children involved, and women tend to get us to tap into our emotions. Women will explain why things should be done as they see it, but men have to stand firm in what they truly believe and not appease because it will come back to bite you. The man finds himself looking into the eyes of that woman, hearing her voice, touching and feeling her sensitivity, and taking in her sweet aroma, falling for her God-given existence, and giving in to her, which is okay to a point. We learn early as boys how to treat girls, and then as men, how to treat women, and the on-the-job training early in life can be confusing. All we do at times is say to ourselves damn because we know we're gonna give in.

Then later on, when she puts that lovin' on you properly, you truly get justification for your commitment. Admit it, fellas, we're born suckas and didn't even know it!

Conundrum, number 4 of the four Cs, is the gateway for the ultimate decision of the final direction of your relationship. Turn right for marriage, turn left for being single. Your "conundrum guess" is as good as mine, my brotha, may God's blessings help carry you and yours throughout the rest of your journey.

CHAPTER 3

The Perception of an Understanding

HAVE YOU EVER asked someone a question that only required truth or a lie as an answer, and they hesitate during the response to get the lie straight or they answer quickly never blinking? They then will have that, does it look like "I'm lying" look of stupidity. You really wanna laugh because you know they're busted. But what's really funny is, we sometimes wanna blame others for our own ignorance of certain issues, but it's "you" who failed to ask the questions or inquire about the relationship you were putting together.

Understandings are created out of communication. What is the perception of an understanding? It's what you perceive the understanding to be. That perception shows and tells how you feel, think, see, and conclude, what you think the understanding actually is to you.

If your partner says that they take money management seriously, that actually means more than "bring me back my change!" If your partner says they want to grow together with you, it means more than just getting an apartment and doing the same ole thing on the regular. This chapter was very interesting for me to put together because of the head-scratching conversations I've had that helped me arrive at this chapter. After asking certain questions, I've heard, let me think about that one, or I'll get back to you on that one. I was allowed to ask specific interworking questions about their togetherness. When people fail to ask the proper questions, they can become complacent or comfortable and think that the learning process is over. During new relationships, everyone will not open up and volunteer all the valuable info you may need to make decisions, so you have to ask and then discuss the responses. Maybe your partner has had issues before you met them, so ask them to be truthful when you say, "Tell me something about yourself." You can have clearer understandings if you ask questions such as, "Why did you feel that way? What was your mentality during that time in your life? Where are you now with this? What did you learn?" These type of questions actually helps both parties individually and as a team.

Here are five words that help describe the typical wrong perception: "But I thought you said!"

If you can "hear me," please "listen" to me, and while listening to me, please "pay attention" to me, and after paying attention to me, can you truthfully tell me you understand me. Those are three different elements involved in developing an understanding when people communicate with each other. Your perceptions of the understandings you have in relationships is derived from if you're the type that hears, listens, or pays attention. When quality communication exists in a relationship, you will find a solid relationship where both partners fully understand what they're involved in. You can ask certain people what they have in their relationship, and you sometimes will get hesitation of the confused type, or a transparent story of someone trying to make themselves look or sound good. Relationships can be complicated because of the numerous unconscious situations that must be addressed constantly, while at the same time, trying to live life itself. When parts of a machine or a structure are not maintained properly, those parts become weakened and don't function as effectively as before. The same concept applies in relationships. What we say and do on a regular basis communicate maintenance of that structure called a relationship or marriage. Sometimes we don't know what we don't know; meaning, we haven't recognized or been made aware of all we're about to learn. So when you hear a new thought, opinion, or fact, an understanding may be just around the corner. Paying attention and quality communication are steps in the right direction of having the proper perception of things you need to understand.

We've all heard "Does everyone understand" or "Raise your hand if you don't understand" and you acted as if you were handcuffed. That's a simple sign of freezing up and not expressing yourself to communicate that you don't understand, which in turn leads to a bad perception. If you don't express yourself in relationships, how do you expect your partner to totally understand you the way you want them to? Your perceptions of understandings in your relationship can either be simple or complicated. To have simplicity within an understanding in your relationship takes work. There has to be truth, honesty, trust, teamwork, quality communication, and belief in your partner. If and when those mentioned qualities exist, it becomes simple to know what you have, why you have it, and with whom you have that understanding with.

When I speak with someone or hear someone explain why they don't understand the inadequacies in their situation, I can see and hear people who refuse to accept the "whole truth." They only want to accept and recognize what makes them comfortable and not anything that either proves them wrong or makes their story vulnerable. There are always two sides to an argument, regardless of who's negative. There is also the reality that there is more to one's own story that they may not want to indulge in. Truth be told, we don't always seek all options to solve problems, just what we desire to seek, not exploring all avenues for solutions that we may not be willing to consider. If we also admit how we could have done better or commit to actually doing better in sharing to solve problems, it makes an understanding a lot simpler. It also depends on one's agenda when determining what type of understanding you will have. Complications within an understanding are very easy to achieve. The lack of seriousness or discipline and the improper agenda in a relationship will immediately breed complication. The lack of quality communication and truth in a relationship only enhances a negative understanding, which may in turn confuse some people into believing that they actually do understand. Imagine the look on one's face when they're asked a question about their situation and they can't answer it because they don't really know or understand the relationship they're in. Some of us may have confusing moments in our relationships, and some of us, unfortunately, are just outright confused.

We all believe that what we're trying to explain should be clearly understood simply because it's clear in our minds, and it could well be, but have you really explained it clearly so that it's understood to that particular person? The fact that a perception of an understanding is what you perceive it to be, a combined acknowledgement of an understanding works better for both parties. "Quality communication" is powerful and will guarantee a true understanding, but just talking "at" each other gives you almost nothing. Your partner may not listen or want to see it your way either because of the way you communicated it, or your way simply does not have both parties interests in consideration.

How you perceive situations to be is based upon what you've learned, and how your personal truth tells you it is. The facts of a matter or situation is clear and plain, but if your mentality convinces you that it's different, you would probably have to be persuaded or convinced in some manner to recognize the true facts. What you choose to accept lets you know if you can handle reality. Some of us don't want truth and reality when it's harsh or cold.

We all want people to understand us as an individual, but are you really willing to understand and accept where they're coming from? If you just disregard their thoughts and feelings because they're not yours, what kind of an understanding do you hope to achieve? You may be correct in your points you're making, but if your way of communicating your feelings and beliefs, don't include involvement in a conversation, your points may not have been clear. Let your partner know by acknowledgement what you agree with and disagree with and not try to prove that you're smarter or better than them. When it comes to understandings, it's very important to have an understanding within yourself first so that you're aware of exactly what you want. You want the same of your partner so that a real bond can be solidified without outside influences.

An extreme example of recognizing the perception of an understanding involves having children. Communicating responsibility about protection during sex should be clear as to whether you two will want children or not. How that understanding is perceived should not be complicated. My whole purpose of this chapter is to relate the importance of quality communication to achieve mutual thinking, purpose, or understanding.

Having a child together is an extremely important part of life we all should be prepared for. I still, to this day, see and hear how some women think a child can keep a man, and I feel it's an emotional thought process a woman goes at alone that enables her to confirm such thoughts. If that decision is discussed or communicated between the two and an understanding is real, then it makes having children an easier decision. It's obvious in life that men and boys can be cleverly manipulating during pure sex and romantic moments, but when a woman is serious, it's no longer up for discussion about how it's going to be. A man has to believe what that woman tells him with major trust involved if he's not smart enough to use protection consistently.

It's a man's responsibility to think with his "brain" in his head instead of the brain in the head of his penis. When a man is told he's gonna be a father and the possibility of becoming a parent is not discussed thoroughly in a sexual relationship, that's not a good surprise.

A persons perception of any particular issue does not speak for everyone, and sometimes may not be what they think it is, if they don't have the facts correct. We also tend to think most times that others understand us clearly when it's not always the case. It's always better to confirm an understanding with your partner to verify that you both have reached a similar or same conclusion hence the phrase, "Are we on the same page?" An example of an unclear perception of an understanding is when you really don't know what your partner wants or needs. If you assume that he or she thinks like you do or should see things as you do, then maybe you should consider reevaluating those thoughts. As mentioned previously, paying attention allows you to know exactly what those needs are.

The following are important keys to a proper perception of an understanding:

- taking the relationship seriously
- being a good listener
- taking your time
- being responsible
- being accountable
- being appreciative
- being humble
- teamwork
- being a producer

If a person has never accepted the common sense knowledge taught to them about companionship, purpose of structure, and the importance of communication and togetherness in relationships, they find themselves struggling to maintain or understand the functioning of their situations. To have concrete knowledge of who you are is significant and brings stability to the understanding equation. Some people, who are described as "know it alls," seem to have all the answers before you even fully explain yourself or the issue. Experience in life is obviously a factor for knowledge, but sometimes it's used as a crutch to convince one's own self that they have the answers.

"Taking your time," when you consider becoming involved in a relationship is the beginning of the smart decisions for success. Being impatient, as if tomorrow is too late, sends you down the wrong path and makes you not to think smartly. If we make important the "desire to acquire" a mutual understanding, then the chances are excellent that your perception of what's understood will be similar or exact. What you don't want in relationship understandings is someone who says, "Yeah, I guess," and speaks that response seriously. Mature adults who call themselves grown-ups have the proper perceptions of the understandings in their situations, and from that point, it's just a matter of being true to your word.

PAUL SIMMS

CHAPTER 4

Truth, Honesty, and Accountability

HONESTY IS DIGESTIBLE; the truth can make you throw up! And accountability is man's self-sufficient measuring stick.

Although truth and honesty have the same or similar dictionary meanings, in my opinion, their effects are not the same. Honesty can be vague while truth is very direct. My suggestion for truth, honesty, and accountability is not a call for perfection but a simple request to do your best to live life in your relationships the best way possible. This chapter states the seriousness of truth, honesty, and accountability in relationships and why it's important for success in your relationship or marriage. We all have "skeletons in the closet" about something in our lives, so what is revealed and how it is revealed speaks also of privacy and secrecy, and relationship experts have written and spoke of the differences. In my opinion, we all will lie about something to someone at a certain point regardless of the magnitude or circumstances.

Even those who live by truth can be brought back to reality if put in a pressured situation; we're simply not perfect.

The truth is such a simple but complicated thing. It's simple because truth can't be truly challenged. It's complicated because it's not that easy to accept on a regular basis for some. Every once in a while, a man has to tell a woman what she wants to hear or to pacify her because of the emotional drawback that may occur. Truth can be similar to finances—if handled correctly, it helps you live comfortably, if not, then you struggle.

The truth is the truth no matter when you hear it, how, where, or from whom you hear or see it. The mere essence of truth is so strongly desired, but effectively shied away from when it has to be accepted sometimes. If you give an opinion that contains truth and others doubt your opinion, don't change your point of view because someone else doesn't agree.

If by chance you were influenced to see a situation different and you truthfully change your opinion, then don't hesitate to change it. Everyone has the right to change their mind; hopefully, there is honesty involved when one does. Truth in relationships can be different from other truths, so to speak, based upon the emotional effect and seriousness when the heart and mind is affected. Lying to your employer for a needed day off does not affect serious emotional feelings and trust issues; it's only business, compared to calling in to your spouse. You have one spouse, but by the numbers, you're immediately replaced at work because it's just business. Accountability is more important in marriages because you don't have doctor's excuses to cover you.

If you have no truth, honesty, and accountability in your relationship, will there be truth at the altar? The answer is an astounding "Absolutely not!"

I've attended a few weddings in my life, including my own, and have gained knowledge during the actual ceremonies as to why I should take marriage even more seriously. The commitment made to God and your future spouse has to be genuine, not a product of the moment. I know for a fact based upon my experience listening and learning from men of all races and ages that many men don't take that type of commitment as seriously as they should. My fear of God will not allow me to raise my hand to him again and verbally and spiritually commit consciously with obvious untruths. Being honest and upfront about your intentions and expectations does not necessarily dictate a certain direction or outcome, but it does open the door for quality communication for hopeful crystal clear understandings. For a person to actually learn a considerable amount about another takes time, so the biggest disadvantage would be your lack of patience. Some people can be very easily rushed to judgment when we fail to give true value to the power of patience. I'm not in total agreement of getting married before having sex and not knowing that you have sexual compatibility. It takes compatibility in all areas, but sexual displeasure will cause major problems eventually, so truth and honesty is important. I'm not against the philosophy and theory of marriage first; it just doesn't work for me.

In our hearts and minds, we know what the truth is while also knowing how we convincingly say what we want it to be. Notice how people can freelance their thoughts and feelings in conversation and make good points, but when truth is asked or demanded, you get a pause. We say that we don't want to play games or want involvement with anyone who plays games, but when we lie, we're simply playing games. How many times have you said or heard say, "Whatever you do, please don't waste my time," and then turn around and say or hear, "Why am I wasting my time with this MF!" In my opinion, we hold on to relationships with little meaning as if we're really about to lose something special, but the situations worth working and fighting for can get less effort.

I have no problem saying up front to women I meet that I'm noncommittal and run the risk of being denied friendship rather than playing games and dealing with unnecessary drama. The truth is realized within us early on; it's accepting it or revealing it to others that can become a problem. Separation or break-ups are not always the best or ultimate solutions to our issues, but why live life with someone who does not take you seriously? Communication that has us talking at each other and constantly criticizing halts progress, so after you make your points with facts, be prepared to offer solutions that work for both parties. Sometimes we dissolve potentially good, or very important relationships involving complete families, based on pettiness and selfishness and refuse to give it one more chance. Problems give us an out we believe we want, but we also recognize that we don't want to lose a good thing until it's too late. Our relationship demise can be dictated by thinking that our own importance is bigger than any rational thinking.

For all involved, say what you mean and mean what you say. Women should tell men what their true expectations are and men should let women know what their true intentions are. We all fall short, and making mistakes is inevitable, but being truthful, honest, and accountable afterward for problem solving is priceless. Truth, honesty, and accountability are also game changing when the truth is about behavior that's absolutely unacceptable. The question is, "Why did you act that way in the first place?" That's the beginning of coming to a solution, which is being able to say why you are, who you are. If you lie about your negative actions naturally, you run the risk of becoming a habitual liar about your actions. Admit your mistakes and explain your guilt in an apology, or truthfully say why you act the way you do. Don't live your relationship in a lie even in the face of others to appear okay as if you're Jekyll or Hyde. If someone tells you they don't want commitment, take them seriously because there's a reason they're telling you that. If and when you make a decision to proceed anyway, you have to be true to yourself in accepting their faults as you see them because "you were warned!" Don't be afraid to make a tough decision if you've been given a decision by your partner and the ball is now in your court. If it's not working, recognize your self-worth and make the tough decision that's better for you. Some of our best decisions are generally unpopular. Now that the ball's in your court, don't go out of bounds.

I've been labeled as being truthful and upfront since my teen years, but I've had my moments of being human and saying what I thought some women wanted to hear. I most definitely had my moments of being sneaky to achieve my goals with women, and I'm proud of it. Fellas, those bullshit games are not really necessary if you're man enough to call it what it really is, and let her know exactly what you want. Having real game or swagger is knowing what and how to say what's needed. Now, there's a line to be drawn between keeping a relationship together that you don't want to lose, and a relationship that has ran its course and you don't want to come to grips with it. Some people need a pat on the back for motivation, others need a kick in the ass. What category do you fall in? You can't actually get better in your relationship unless you apply yourself to get better, so if you don't get off your ass and do what it takes to be better, it's not going to happen.

Women say they want a man who will just be truthful, and rightly so, but remember, ladies, that it's a two-way street. "A woman's confusion makes a man's world complicated." I state that in the context, men are basic and simple, and women tend to analyze or over-analyze issues and simple things. A man's thinking is so basic that it either works or it doesn't, where women will talk about why, because, if, about, compared to, alternatives, and how it affects their feelings. Believe it or not, but those two differences help off-set each other in relationships between men and women, and it's a good thing. Now let's not deny the truth about some women's agenda to acquire men for specific reasons such as security.

There's absolutely nothing wrong with women having those feelings and expectations, just be woman enough to admit it. "Fair exchange is no robbery"! As long as there is a mutual understanding based upon being open and true about why you're together, no one can counterclaim the righteousness and reality only you two and God truthfully have established. On the other hand, the truth is that, if you're lying to your partner deep down inside about serious and real issues and you get upset at them because they're not doing something up to your standards, think about how fake and unreal you're both living in your relationship or marriage.

An age-old question of relationship truth is the question women ask, "What do men really want?" This question has been asked and answered generation after generation. My thoughts, feelings, philosophy, and theory to answer the question boils down to the basic answers. A man's first or initial thought is sexual—plain and simple. But now let's ask, is that all that he really wants? The real question is what does he want from you? A man can speak to women all day, but you in particular, Ms. Lady, is where the real issue lies. As men, we know what we want, which is actually what we don't want—commitment to one woman. Some men won't agree with that perspective, and I guarantee you that they've found that "one." Ladies, when you're looking for truth, honesty, and accountability in a man, here's an explanation of how men may appear to "not know" what they want. We can have one woman but have sexual desires for another woman, or be single and still won't settle for one as well. See, the part about being instinctively promiscuous is very real, and wanting to be with one woman is a process. True love in a man's heart will stop him cold in his tracks, guaranteed. To conquer more than one woman is a testosterone issue men are born with, so it has to be difficult for some women to understand that of a man, which she can't feel. If it doesn't make sense to you, it can't be easily acceptable. Men know they want multiple women; it's not confusing to us at all. The confusing part is when that "one" woman appears in our life at any given moment, and we temporarily lose the macho control we're so proud of. We instantly know in our heart that we're about to transform our thought process and our outlook. Suddenly, having many women is no longer important, pleasing the most important one takes extreme precedence over any and all others.

To be truthful, we deeply respect a man who loves, respects, and dedicates his life to his family; it's a beautiful thing. Having a family he has provided happiness to and lives in is more important because it has more meaning, purpose, and is more fulfilling. In my opinion, no man can truthfully claim to be faithful for a lifetime because no man can predict that many years of change in his future with the natural promiscuous trait in our gender, plus temptation. There are always exceptions to rules, but in this case, it would be a true rarity. If a man's truly in love, he will be strong and valiant in his effort, but the desire to conquer is naturally instilled, and time is the biggest enemy. The strength in his spiritual faith and strong desire to please his God can also guide him. Men are natural creatures of show, being a braggadocio in such manners as a Herculean body, my woman is finer than yours, my home and vehicle is nicer than yours, my money is bigger, as well as my sensual stimulus package. When a man has hormonal infatuation toward women, he's still being led by his promiscuity.

"Just be accountable" is the motto I absorbed years ago after becoming tired of dodging issues and truth in my many short-term relationships. It doesn't matter if it's your words or actions, stand for what you've said or done as if you truly mean it because you meant it when you said it or done it. If you didn't mean it, then stand behind why you lied about it. There's truth in accountability when you own up to who, what, and how you are. You may feel embarrassment sometimes for the consequences of stating accountability, but confidence helps you stay strong and convicted about being real. Your confidence convinces others that your ability to handle the truth, truly defines your purpose. There's respect, admiration, and appreciation from others toward you when you're accountable because it shows you're serious about yourself, and respect begins with self. When we say, "I don't wanna talk about it," we either just wanna give up on the topic, or we've been exposed. If we put as much effort into quality in relationships as we do in hobbies like sports and shopping, imagine the success rate and less need for counseling.

Being accountable also means making up your own mind while you're thinking for yourself. Receiving advice or help from those you trust are good supplements, but we still have to make the final decisions for our own destiny in life, and it's what decisions you actually make that justifies your accountability and daily functioning. However, please be aware and careful when receiving advice because there's a difference between advice and directives. Our ability to make up our own minds is unfortunately worsening based upon the magnitude of unqualified outlets of opinions available. That gives us many manipulated opinions. Some people truly believe that all the answers to questions are in their computers, deleting their brain and heart. Remember the cliché "Use your head," well, hell, now that seems like too much work. First the calculator, now the personal computer, what's next? I-Robot!

If you're not about being accountable, or you've noticed that you haven't been, consider looking seriously into living your life in an accountable manner. Don't say you're about accountability and you work or talk your way out of what's real about what you say or do especially when you're wrong. Being accountable means you have integrity, and that's something to be proud of. Blaming others for your mistakes is not a sign of being accountable obviously, but you can truly see how good it feels to admit what you've said or done regardless of what it is.

Try it sometime to see how it feels and works, and if you have real issues with lying, you probably will seriously stop lying as much. There's a big difference in what we actually do or feel in relationships compared to what we should be doing.

Relationships have been challenged with the aspect of two heads of households or confused equality. An example of an oxymoron is an alpha male and an independent woman coexisting and functioning happily in a seriously committed relationship. That would be similar to antifreeze in an engine, it's just a matter of time before it lock's up! I'm sure I will be challenged by some on this issue, but in my opinion, you may not be as alpha or independent as you claim if there's minimum issues. The term *independent woman* automatically defines her lack of need for dependency, which immediately begins relationship demise. I understand *independent* refers to being solo, but in our society, the cliché speaks for itself. True independent women are strong with secure mentalities and strong work ethics because they're doing what has to be done, solo. Having success while being independent promotes individuality, and it will take the truest alpha male to get her to drop her guards, her way of life depends on it. But how could these two coexist when the alpha male functions with a mind-set that dares anyone to question his position unless he allows it, and the independent woman is standing tough with an aura that says, "I can do it with you or without you!" Committing to each other and accepting who, what, and how they are is paramount because compromise should rule decision making until some tables are turned. Accountability will be very present in such type of relationships because of both partners being confident and proud. But she will let her guard down and commit and submit if the proper man proves his worth. An alpha male as well will calm his demeanor to a woman he's in love with if she respects him and doesn't challenge his manhood.

One of my defining moments of my becoming accountable was accepting the fact that I've been hurt in my life and admitting that it was hard to get over. I lived with it for a long time as it affected me, but being accountable has freed my mind, heart, and soul to say it's okay. Being accountable has allowed me to become more accepting and to start taking responsibility. I've taught my young daughter about the importance of self-respect and hope that, as life goes on for her, she will make herself important and not rely on anyone else to do it for her. Confidence and pride will strengthen with self-respect and accountability and make correct decisions easier to arrive at for anyone if you realize it and accept it. Strong accountability traits involve knowing what you have and who you are and not being confused about what you want out of life. Once you have stability mentally, then you can be accountable for all your actions and words. I have contentment in my life because I have peace. I have peace because I'm drama free. I make being drama free very important and try not to get involved with people who wish to involve me in it. It's a blessing from God to have it this way, but I put myself in this comfortable state.

I value truth, honesty, and accountability and rank them high in priorities and as standards, so I have only small personal issues to deal with.

After a pattern of inconsistency in remaining committed to relationships for various reasons, I realized that I was more content being single. The truth is, I have no desire for commitment because I'm not in love. I'm tired of having committed relationships that I know in my heart I have no future in, and I don't want to lie to pacify feelings. When I'm up front and when I come clean from the get-go, it's a very comfortable feeling and I realize I'm not missing out on anything. Women also truly appreciate truth in the beginning, which allows them to make an informed decision. When it comes to making decisions about me, there's no one to challenge me about what's important to me. I could be living my life based on what someone else's vision of my happiness should be, but no, I create and live my happiness. I do understand sharing in life with your soul mate, but sharing and intrusion are two different things.

I enjoy being who I am and being accepted for it, not being told how I should be or why I do what I do. Doing what I want to do, when I want, how I want, where I want, and with whom I want, is basically relationship freedom. That type of freedom is very important to me either as a single man or if I'm involved in a relationship. You notice the reaction of anticipation a dog has when they see you coming to release them from their leash or when you open a door. That feeling of freedom is so exhilarating that they run as fast as they can in whatever direction regardless of where they may end up. Well, I wanna run like a MF until I pass out, just to know I don't have any restrictions. I understand completely that in a committed relationship, you don't have complete freedom and understandibly so, but I'm not comfortable with being given ultimatums or restrictions, or asking for permission. The thing is, you have to have the accountability to do what's right for your family "first," and then be yourself, "which is truly not complicated." Being monogamous is just as fulfilling, if not more, when you commit to the right person for the right reasons. Fellas, don't multitask by having a family and trying to be a male whore, that's a true sign of immaturity or selfishness; make up your mind and quit wasting everyone's time. Men simply need to also make their minds up about what kind of men they are, how they should and will be, and live it with conviction.

Another aspect of being accountable is knowing what you're about to get involved in, so asking the proper questions is imperative. Along with the normal, what do you do? Ask about mood swings, being involved in or attending events that's not normally your style, how one feels about drugs, future family, work habits, spirituality, finances, education, and health concerns. Personal and semipersonal topics will be touched depending on how serious one plans to be.

My auntie taught me, "A closed mouth doesn't get fed," and that applies also to your hunger for knowledge.

Internet dating or "computer love" seems to be very popular. Match dating seems reasonable when trying to find compatibility if there's truth and accountability in your profile. Telling a lie at a bar, church, grocery store, Laundromat, or on a computer is no different, they're all bullshit lies. Be accountable for what you say in your profile however or whenever you present it. The test of being accountable by one example is accepting one who has a past that's not acceptable by your love ones. Whether it was drugs, crime, prostitution, or bad health, it truly depends on the strength you have in you and the level of accountability within to handle these type situations. The comfort of explaining to your partner and to those whose opinions you value is different if there is a suspicious past to explain. We need to know one's real past in order to have a real future.

Some secrets should be kept secret, and some should be revealed depending on how your partner can be affected. Privacy on the other hand will be jeopardized eventually, so be prepared for it. Fellas, be accountable for being the man to her and treat her as such. If you're not feeling it, then dig deeper within to find it if you know she's worth it to you.

Accountability is achieved when we accept exactly what the circumstances are, and have the integrity to stand alone and be truthful. Some very important relationships or marriages fail to blossom into their best because of a stubbornness to want to prove their partner at fault versus debating to solve the issue as a team. Think about it, how can you truly expect a relationship to improve or grow if you believe that your partner is the only one who needs to realize how wrong they are so, "just be accountable"? If we could just try to consider what and why they feel the way they do and be considerate of why it's important to them, you can then work toward solving issues together through quality communication. Give your commitment what it truly deserves.

CHAPTER 5

Who I Am, What I Am, How I Am Can You Accept Me for Me?

AT SOME POINT in your life someone has asked, "Who are you," similar to the lyrics of the titled song by the rock band the Who. This chapter contains three important ways of focusing to determine who, what, and how someone actually is. They are the acceptance of, the understanding of, and the allowance of. A lot of people will automatically stereotype while not knowing what's actual, and in my opinion, stereotyping is an unspoken admission of true ignorance.

Accepting someone for who, what, and how they are takes time. The whole concept of building a successful relationship has everything to do with choosing and accepting the right person first and foremost, so getting to know them thoroughly is paramount. You may never get to know who a person is if you refuse to accept them for who, what, and how they are. People sometimes try to create a new mind-set or behavior pattern within other people before knowing why a person thinks, acts, and functions as they do. We're so busy trying to prove how smart we are, we can sometimes do or say unnecessary things, or we just simply forget the basics. When your thoughts and your tongue are quick to dismantle a person through judgment and belittlement because they don't think or act like you, then you may never truly know that person, understand them, or persuade them otherwise. It's a beautiful thing to share your knowledge with someone else in an attempt to help better them, but your approach has to be correct in order to be truly accepted and respected.

Once you find out what a person is, you make a decision to accept it or you plot to change it. When you find out how they are, you make a decision that you're convinced you either can or can't deal with that type personality and behaviors. Once you find out who a person is, you make a decision that deals with being compatible and if they fit what you want in life. All these decisions are separate and take time to understand fully unless you make the time to invest. The old-school R & B group the Staple Singers had a verse in a song called "Respect Yourself" that said, "You're walking around acting like the world owes you something because you're here, you're going out the world backward like you did when you first come here, respect yourself!" It's a classic example of those who feel as if we're done learning at times, or that we're so much better than others, which breaks down your ability to learn who someone truly is. In all actuality, you can't learn anything with your mouth open and your ears, eyes, and mind closed.

How do we define who, what, and how we are? In my opinion, who we are describes us as parents of our children, children of our parents, siblings, and friends. What I am describes gender, ethnicity, career or profession, hobbies, or addictions. How I am describes one's personality traits and behaviors or emotional makeup, such as passion, spirituality, shyness, temper, sociability, passiveness, or aggressiveness. So when we find ourselves in a position to get to know someone, looking at these particulars or specific characteristics is important if you're trying to build a relationship with meaning. Who, what, and how we are describe our values, principles, and morals. If you don't take time to analyze what you have and seek improvement and progression for stability and longevity, then what's your real purpose in the relationship. If it's for one or two things specifically, then make sure it's understood; asking questions about one's past will give you an idea of how they were raised, and how they came to develop their standards and values. We are who we are and should be accepted as such, but keep in mind that time brings about change.

Patience and time will reveal who one is because no one can fake it every single day. Personally, I can appreciate a woman with an opinion and who is willing to express it. I prefer a woman who will show and tell me what her worth is about. I can spoil a woman to a point, but I refuse to allow her to command or demand what I should do for her unless she has proved to me she's that one I must invest my all in. Neither a man nor a woman should sign their life away to someone who hasn't proven inevitable staying power because regrets can be a bitch sometimes. I don't see success with a woman who competes with me about who's running things—that should be a shared process of communicating. Men should always come strong when needed but should respect that woman's position, her opinions, values, and desires.

Ladies, when you decide to have that relationship and you accept him, can you allow that man to be who he is, what and how he is, and you can still have genuine fun with him? Or do you feel embarrassed about his ways on a regular basis or have to defend his actions. If it's a problem, address it at a later time by asking him to represent the family or the relationship with mutual respectful behavior. Please don't ask "at" him to allow for rebellion. If he loves you and respects you, he will realize his mistakes. Some people in relationships enjoy life because they're being themselves while their partner goes through life not living their own life, trying to cater to their partner's personality. Being incarcerated in your relationship by having someone directly or indirectly manipulate your daily functioning is not fun, so find your moment and express yourself to your partner about what's important to you, and how you prefer they accept you as you. If you recognize your relationship as full of assumptions instead of real understanding, address it. Try to have a welcomed working relationship with your partner.

Often in conversations, when I hear people say that they don't understand certain aspects of their relationship or marriages, it makes me think of the work put into communicating an understanding of what they actually have. Do you really know who you're with, and do you accept how they are and what they are? If you don't accept their values and behaviors, it's time to reevaluate your own values again to see why you're in it. I've taken notice of and have held conversation with men who allow women to dictate what direction in life they're heading in. Women can give good advice about basic life principles, family structure, values and more, but telling a man how to conduct himself as a man is as ridiculous as the man receiving that advice. "Grow a Pair" is the slogan appropriate for that scenario.

If you're in a situation where you're deciding to change from a good friendship, to try to begin a committed relationship, that's a very serious line to cross. You two may know each other well being friends, so if there was a genuine interest at the very beginning and it progressed, God be with you. If you're settling to satisfy a curiosity, don't do it. True friendship is better than short-lived sex. Manufacturing relationships is the same as looking for love and searching for it. Be yourself and live life to the fullest.

There are, sometimes, particular requirements and obligations involved in order to maintain a relationship with some people. When you meet them and spend time getting to know them, you learn what those requirements are, and at that point, your decisions will affect how you plan on functioning, or so you think. One thing's for sure; it's not easy to change. Adjustments are easier to make because it's more give and take and does not totally take away from who you are. When you have no problem sharing in life, adjustments are just a part of sharing. If you truly have a problem with those issues up front, don't hesitate to communicate that you handle life differently. If someone prefers high quality material assets and you're simpler in life, who will change? If one's spiritual preferences are different, being equally yoked goes to topic number one.

Here's a tip for women to consider. When trying to figure out what can make your man happy, look at what's important to him specifically and how it makes him react when it goes good. For those type of guys who love football and are blessed enough to have their team play in a very important game such as the Super Bowl, watch a man's anticipation for success and how bad he wants it. The moment his team scores a touchdown in the final moments of a close game that seals the deal for a win, you will see emotions exposed that may surprise you and will help explain who, what, and how he is. If you can accept that about him and allow him to enjoy that important aspect of his life, he will truly respect you for it. Sports may not be the only important aspect that means that much, but if you can accept the most important things that are his "makeup" then you are accepting him for who, what, and how he is. There is a difference between just simply dealing with someone's important aspects of life and truthfully accepting it. That man should accept and respect you in that same manner for what's most important in life to you as well.

Some people can be demanding and some can be commanding with only a slight difference between the two. Being commanding means to give direct orders to function or behave in a particular manner, and being demanding means you ask with authority having no alternative. You must recognize these two characteristics, and which one if they exist and how it will affect you. They both show a dominant or controlling behavior pattern with arrogance, but it also depends on one's total personality whether they're the type that ask you or tell you what to do. There's actual respect for controlled commanding or demanding such as a coach or drill instructor, and little respect for those who manipulate with those traits. If one of these traits is present when you decide to begin a relationship, you have to know that you can truly accept it. Sometimes it's difficult to make choices between your heart and your mind about accepting a person for who, what, and how they are. Clouded judgment can cause difficulty in determining the difference between love and fascination.

Ladies, allow your man the proper opportunity to prove he can be the leader of your family. If he can't in your opinion, then communicate positive adjustments or changes. Fellas, don't control your family, lead your family but control your children's direction. If the proper togetherness is original and genuine, then all is good, but if power struggles exist or develop, communicating to solidify a worthwhile relationship is well worth it. If there's a major decision to be made and you two can't compromise, who makes the decision? For some women, it can be like swallowing a bowling ball to decide to let a man be the deciding factor and make head of the family decisions, as it should be. Always maintain who you really are and how you are by not dumbing yourself down to level the playing field trying to justify your togetherness. Help educate or persuade your partner to vision how it can be better overall with a different approach. When your own personal level of communicating begins to lack quality, don't expect anyone to understand and accept you because you more than likely are talking at each other than to each other. When I hear "He/she just don't understand me," well, I wonder why. Failure to communicate properly does not allow you to know who you're dealing with, how they truly are, and what they're truly about in different situations. It's not a good thing if an outsider knows your inner relationship and your partner better than you.

"Going through the motions are for machines, not human beings."

Try to understand that there's a difference between forced involvement and persuaded involvement. When you give your partner space to be him or herself, you help create a comfort level to be utilized for self-worth, and when it feels good to be yourself, it will show in your relationship. Forced involvement stems from manipulation or fear. When we do things we absolutely despise just to appease others, your relationship either stalls or takes a step backward. When you make someone miserable while satisfying your personal feelings and you're good with it, it's wrong. On the other hand, persuasion is a good thing because there's satisfaction on both sides.

If within midstream of your relationship, you feel and recognize that there is personal change within you, it's vital to communicate what, how, and why the importance of your transformation to your partner because total change can and will change your level of togetherness. To have someone believe and know you're one way and then change, you have to allow your partner the option to accept it or not. No one is obligated to accept whatever you accept, and thinking that they should is wrong. When we have a desire to be with someone for a particular reason, we go blind to the fact that they have many other qualities about them we haven't considered, and later on, you'll wonder why there are problems. If you meet someone who's into drugs, crime, or disrespectful behavior and you have a fascination for the bad boy aura, be aware of the choices you've made. Don't blame him for being a bad boy later, or don't blame her for being high maintenance if that's her style from day one.

If you want your partner to be involved in what you're about, it's a lot easier to create a more comfortable and attractive environment in order to convince your partner about your way of thinking and why it's important to you so that their interest becomes greater. No matter what you're doing, if you do it in a manner that seems interesting, others will follow to a point. Ladies, if you ever wonder whether a man needs you or not, yes, he does—to partner with in many areas of his life, to benefit him, but not to be changed into something he has absolutely no interest in. For all involved, a manufactured interest you create for someone else is not real until that person genuinely accepts it; until then, it's all fake.

If a relationship could be compared to a corporation by structure, the man should be considered the CEO (chief executive officer), and the woman would be the COO (chief operating officer). The CEO is the head man in charge and is solely responsible for making sure everyone has everything needed to do their part to keep it together such as the home, education, rules, values, principles, purposes, discipline, food, and security. If anything goes wrong, the CEO is the one to blame if he does not get it back on track. It all falls back on the CEO who takes on that title because he says he's the man who can handle the job. Now let's talk about the one with the real power, the COO. In order for the family or relationship to actually function, and the shots are called on a daily basis as to what's really goin' on, the COO does that without hesitation. The COO may have a title a step below CEO, but trust and believe who's really in charge of this situation. The cliché "He who has the gold makes the rules" stands true here because the COO is the extremely valuable commodity of this situation; she's Momma! Men do realize the strength, power, and presence we bring in a relationship, but being knocked down a peg is inevitable once the right woman arrives in his life. That's who she is, what she is, and how she is, period.

If you genuinely take the time to understand your partner, you will learn who and how they are and know if it's okay to accept them as such and then allow them to be themselves. If a successful relationship is what you're developing, trying to keep, or you're repairing, true knowledge of who you're working with gives you a winning hand!

CHAPTER 6

The Mirror Is for More than Grooming

WHEN IN THE mirror you can't lie, there's nowhere to hide, so please don't try!

We prep, flex, correct, direct, and check for fat spots, bald spots, wet spots, and missing parts, while at the same time we inhale and exhale for temporary glory. The moment you see yourself in the mirror, you will know truly whether you should be proud of yourself or how fake you're being in life. The power of a mirror can cause that same mirror to be cherished or destroyed, depending on the emotions involved at that moment. It's okay to make mistakes in life, so don't judge yourself too harshly and know that you can only control what you can control. If diamonds are a woman's best friend, does mirrors make the top three or top five for women, which probably includes shoe shopping, gifts of love, or a good man; and no, ladies, the latter is not an oxymoron.

The concept behind this chapter is to get one to understand and realize that, as you actually use a mirror every day, you can truly take time to have a mental conversation containing true therapeutic importance of yourself. So whether you need to seek professional help or just simply apply personal strength to improve your situation, it begins with you. The mirror can obviously reflect external images good or bad, but it can truly reflect, as well, internal happiness or pain. You can hold a conversation in the mirror without moving your lips; it's the focus mentally to either get your point across to gain confidence or to get that person who is your reflective twin to come to an obvious realization. Your image in the mirror changes every single time you come back to it, but it's what's in your soul that remains the same. However, serious soul-searching for change requires very serious self analyzing, and some may find that type change once or twice in a lifetime.

As we proceed, this chapter also should bring awareness to self-worth, self-respect, self-reliance, and being true to yourself. Just like it's easy and simple to go to the gym for your physical health, take your mind to the mental gym for healthier access. Your mentality is just as important as your physical, so make sure you make adjustments or changes as well if necessary. If your feelings about your life changes drastically, you can see it in the mirror, so the cliché "Check yourself before you wreck yourself" would be a true conscious evaluation of the standards that you've set for yourself and your direction. In order to maintain or improve your standards, do a "for real" mental check instead of skimming through your thoughts. If you want to be taken serious, then become serious. The mirror is for more than grooming.

Self-image is so important to women that, a ten-inch by three-inch mirror hanging from a windshield at sixty miles an hour has become a standard, ergonomic, operating vehicle option. Image can be the deciding factor why one even approaches another to try to begin a friendship or relationship, so the physical image in the mirror has to be right because you never know who you'll meet. Self evaluation gives you the opportunity to examine your life's commitment, your spirituality, values, security, and your health. Think about the decisions you will have to make with the end result as the main focus, and how it should benefit you. When in that mirror, ask yourself, what are my standards and values, and do I hold myself to them? You hear the cliché, "I'm just gonna do me," in which, if you decide that for your life, then don't procrastinate. Be serious about your situation and make "you" important this time. If you keep saying it and never do it, then you might as well get a part-time job blowing up balloons with all that hot air you're wasting. The person in the mirror has to know that the change in them comes from their own importance. If change makes you a better person, you should be a better partner in your relationship. Walk proud and step with confidence knowing exactly what you're all about, for real. Get your money right by just simply having access to money at any moment. We all want to be rich or well off, but it's not really how much you make or have, it's how you save and spend it as well as your approach to be successful such as investments. Find a career or profession and go for it regardless of how minor some may look at it. People will respect you for at least doing something, which goes well with self-pride. Remember to do your best and let God take care of the rest.

It's a fact that women mature faster than men, but that's not an excuse for men to delay their maturity. Accepting responsibility makes you mature while doing what it takes to do the right thing for all involved, not just doing responsible things sometimes. That mirror will help you realize what's important to you, and you have to dig deep down inside to exercise truth and honesty and show and tell the world who you are. If others don't accept the truth from you, keep confident in your discovery of what's true about you. If you truly value your confidant's opinion, ask for it without allowing them to make decisions for you; there's a chance you may hear something you can't see. A new you should allow you to accept your strengths and weaknesses for what they are and improve on them. Whatever your best communication skills are, there's someone out there who is truly interested in what you have to say. Have patience, be yourself and express yourself, and they will arrive eventually. Have you ever told someone you're not a materialistic person, and then turn right around and judge someone based upon what they have or don't have? We all at some point will judge or grade people based upon what we think their collection of materialistic assets should be or their level of worth, but that does not necessarily make you materialistic because you could be just simply making an assessment or observation, but when you start judging for what they "should" have as far as particulars, that's when your materialistic faults show. Being in denial about certain aspects or behaviors in your life or your personality in general is another reason to know that the mirror is for more than grooming. The acceptance of truth and reality is the therapeutic remedy we're looking for here.

Please know and recognize that there's someone great and important in all of us, it's all in who accepts you for you. As you stand before that mirror, ask yourself, what's more influential, the heart or the mind? Your heart is what houses your emotions, and it doesn't matter whether they're high-end frustrating or simply telling you how beautiful love is. Your mind is the facilitator of your actions derived from your emotions, and you will be judged by your words and actions. I personally believe that what's truly in your heart and soul shapes your personality, and your mind will inform you on how to carry out your functions. A person's mind can be changed by someone else, but only you can truly change your heart. What's in your heart is truly you because it's what you feel in your soul, and that's why you should be who "you" are and not what someone else wants you to be.

The person in the mirror should be your biggest ally outside your faith in God.

Being an older gentleman, time and experience has awarded me more appreciation and respect for women as well as a better understanding of them. I've always had respect for women because that's how I was raised. For the young men who think and feel that they've got it down totally, imagine what you will learn in the next twenty-five years compared to what you've already learned so far. As you stand before that mirror, take pride in knowing that there's much to learn and how much better you can and will be. It should be simple for men to realize and recognize that when your woman's appearance changes, something is going on emotionally or mentally, and a possible "lack" of attention and appreciation on your part will be handled by another man or woman.

What she wants in her own relationship with you has been either diluted or deleted, and she wants to be loved and shown that she still means everything to you. Remember that the strength in your relationship is based upon what you decide to bring to it. She may not have been the only one to have changed, especially if something in your personal world has taken up significant importance to you. If it's sports, money, a woman, work, or a deep disagreement within your relationship, that negative change can and should be handled. Look in that mirror, take a deep breath, and then go through the truth of the problem, then go through the truth for the best solution. Before you walk away from that mirror, the answer should be in front of you. Don't be opposed to asking for a second opinion or bouncing things off a confidant or friend to arrive at a solution.

Confusion is a normal human state of the mind that happens sometimes, but it has to be overcome, and the mirror is a place to give yourself good advice about reality. We tend to open up and express our feelings to friends, family, and strangers, but then when we're eye to eye with our partner, our lips and tongue go numb to the truth. Our partners would just die to hear how and what we think and how we truly express ourselves elsewhere detail for detail, learning your true emotional state and feelings, the exact same way that you express in the mirror to your reflective twin. If and when you see raw emotion, that's when you know in your heart that a solution becomes priority one. You may not be able to see your heart in the mirror, but it sure as hell can be felt. The mirror is for more than grooming.

Ladies, there's a difference between what a man drools over as sexy or as easy and how and if he respects you for being sexy. A woman will receive respect and appreciation if she carries herself in such a manner that demands it. If a woman is feeling flirtatious sexy that day and dresses the part, then we know who let the dogs out at that point. A hungry dog just wants to be fed, he could care less about what the fancy bowl is made of; meaning, he doesn't directly care what you're really all about at that moment, it's about the best strategy to get some, and any man can just want some when he meets you, but his perception of you will direct how he will approach and respect you and all that depends on you. Your representation of yourself can and will actually tame that dog. He can't and won't be fed, until you allow him to! In all actuality, a man who cares will make providing, securing, and protecting you as important to him as you make it important to yourself. The mirror will reflect that appearance, and the truth about how you want those dogs to bark!

I realize and admit that I can't tell you what to do; I'm just trying to offer relationship considerations. We all will look for angles to find solutions for relationship dilemmas, and I try to simply state what could be considered. We all make decisions based upon our own personal makeup, which eventually defines us. As you stand before that mirror of life, the reflection in that mirror is you! You control the direction and the purpose of which is you, so take a moment to ponder change if it's necessary or give yourself credit if it applies. It takes two to make it work (even when you're before that mirror), so take a moment to recognize what you're truly and truthfully bringing to the table. If you feel you are truly wasting your time in your current situation, then how long are you going to allow it to continue? Whenever you get through, it's about self-respect and self-responsibility and making yourself happy first and foremost. If you allow someone else to drag you backward, don't blame it all on them, point the finger at the one in the mirror. Relationships or marriages will never be easy to maintain; it takes a lot of work, but they should be more simplistic rather than complicated over time. The proper way to maintain relationships comes with two sets of instructions, the one's you've been taught and the one's you've taught yourself, and once you understand the instructions, you then begin to build your solid foundation with the proper materials and keep up your insurance of assurances that you will rebuild after every strong storm or catastrophe that damages your foundation. Remember, the stories that you hear in the mirror are not ones that you've heard elsewhere, they're the one's you've created, so get the story right!

PAUL SIMMS

CLOSING

HOW DO WE define relationship success? Individually, we have varying degrees on how we measure success whether we're speaking of ourselves or others. And as I've previously mentioned, we're only human and will make our mistakes while we handle our business in a manner we believe fits us. I can only have hope, along with my personal desire, that my book will enlighten and legitimately help someone in their search for relationship success. Always "PLAY TO WIN", while doing your best to manage the mental, the emotional, and the physical aspects of your situations in relationships that occur time after time, knowing that it's not easy to do for everyone. To the men, my "FOUR C's" are my way of saying that there's a 4 step process that can be handled either positively or negatively, and while in the "barbershop", dont hesitate to express your opinion on how it's supposed to go in order to begin another hot topic of the day. And Ladies, while at the salon please feel free to explain or expose what you feel men know or dont know about the "FOUR C's. (that should not be difficult for some) For all involved, I will be very interested to know that after giving importance to your perceptions of your understandings, crystal clear knowledge of what was meant, is now what you look for. TRUTH BE TOLD! is what I also hope becomes a part of some of our revised standards, such as, "Im standing up for mine and being accountable"! I know who he is! I know what she is! And we know how we are, because that's how it's supposed to be, is what we've accomplished here ladies and gentlemen. Do you have a "Favorite Mirror"? Well, now you have a new outlook from some of those visits in that same mirror because now you're groomed up, schooled up, and you've moved up! The King of Hearts, for you my Lord, your Queen awaits, and for you my Lady, Madame Queen of Diamonds, your King awaits you! . . . . GOD BLESS YOU ALL!

www.ingramcontent.com/pod-product-compliance
Lightning Source LLC
Chambersburg PA
CBHW031327290526
45784CB00014B/2357